A NEW BEST FRIEND AT SIENA FARMS

ISBN-13: 978-0-578-87492-0
Published by Lyndon Haviland Publishing
Illustration: Sarah Neff
Design: Mario M. Muller
Printed in the United States of America

For all the friends who
light up our lives.

Farmer Chris had a secret.
It was a surprise for Chef Ana and Siena.
Farmer Chris told Siena,
"Close your eyes, hold out your hands!"

Farmer Chris put a puppy in Siena's arms.
"Her name is Rory. She will be our new best friend!"

Rory was small but wiggly. She was ginger colored with floppy ears, big paws and a tail that would not stop moving. Rory ran around the house and smelled everything.

She crawled under the couch. She ran down the hallway.
She sat at the bottom of the stairs and looked up.
Rory was not sure about the stairs.

Rory followed Farmer Chris all over the house.
She even braved going up the stairs.
She did not want to let Farmer Chris out of her sight.

Rory loved upstairs. There were shoes and clothes and plants to explore. It was so exciting and so exhausting.
Rory lay down in a pile of Farmer Chris's boots to take a nap. A sunbeam shone on her as she slept.

At night, Rory slept on the floor
next to Farmer Chris and Chef Ana's bed.
Rory liked nighttime. It was quiet and the moon shone bright.
She could hear the owls hooting.
The owls seemed far away, almost as far as the moon.

Rory did not like thunder or lightning.
The noises and the bright flashes scared her. When thunder
boomed, Rory flattened herself under the bed and wouldn't

In the morning, Rory liked to put her paws on the windowsill and watch as Siena went off to school.

Rory liked to follow Chef Ana into the kitchen.
It smelled so good.
She sat right under Chef Ana's feet.

When Chef Ana turned to the stove,
Rory put her nose up to the counter.

Rory grabbed a bone and ran.
Chef Ana chased her.
Rory liked this game.

"Oh, Rory! Look what you've done! Now, drop the bone. That's a good dog," said Chef Ana. Rory was sad. She put her head on the floor.

Rory watched Farmer Chris leave for the barn.

Rory barked and barked some more.
Chef Ana was not happy.
Farmer Chris was not happy. Rory was not happy.

Rory did not want to stay home.
She wanted to go outside with Farmer Chris.

One sunny day,
Farmer Chris took Rory out to the barn.
Rory was happy. She danced around Farmer Chris.

Farmer Chris wore rubber boots and suspenders. He smelled like dirt and growing things. He smiled whenever he looked at Rory.

Farmer Chris took Rory out to the fields
riding tall on his tractor. Rory liked the fields
and she liked the way the tractor dug holes in the ground.
Rory jumped off the tractor and started digging holes.

Rory liked the fields full of vegetables
and the sunflowers that grew so tall. Everything smelled great
and there were many places to dig and to hide.

Rory liked the rabbits.
She liked to chase them. It was fun!

Rory liked the foxes playing by the stream.
She barked at them to play with her,
but they disappeared.

Rory liked the cool dark mushroom cave.
It was a good place to take a nap,
but Farmer Chris chased her out and closed the door.

Rory liked the barn best of all. Rory liked the barn cat who hissed and ran away. She liked the barn swallows high up in the rafters. She barked at them, and they flew away.

Rory loved to see Legacy and Agnes and their stalls in the barn.
Muddy boots were piled up next to their stalls.
They smelled good!

Legacy was tall. Agnes was round. And Rory was small.

Rory barked at Agnes.

Rory barked at Legacy.
Rory just wanted to be friends.

Legacy looked at Agnes and she looked at Rory.
Then, Legacy turned away.

Agnes dipped her head at Rory and she settled down in her stall.
She closed her eyes.

Rory was sad no one wanted to be her friend. So Rory dug into the pile of boots and started chewing. The boots tasted great. Rory fell asleep.

At the end of the day, Farmer Chris could not find Rory. He looked everywhere but he did not see her sleeping in the pile of boots.

Farmer Chris went home alone.
He was sad. Siena and Chef Ana were sad, too.

The house was quiet.
There was no barking,
no chasing,
no Rory sleeping by the bed.

Rory woke up cold and alone in the pile of boots. The night was dark. Clouds hid the moon. Rory was hungry and scared. The owls hooted as they swept through the barn.

Rory started to cry. Her crying woke up Legacy and Agnes. Legacy turned around towards the sound. Agnes got to her feet. They pushed their heads over the stalls to see who was making so much noise. They saw Rory and they saw she was sad.

Agnes nudged the stall door open. Agnes looked at Rory and Rory looked at Agnes.

Rory pushed herself flat and into Agnes' stall. It was warm and the hay smelled fresh and clean.

Agnes lay down carefully. Rory curled up next to her.
Rory licked her ear. They both fell asleep.
When the sun came up, Farmer Chris found Rory and Agnes
asleep together, safe and happy. He smiled a big smile.

Rory woke with a start and barked with joy to see Farmer Chris.
She gave Agnes a quick lick and jumped into Farmer Chris's arms.

He laughed and said, "Dogs may be our best friend but Legacy
and Agnes will be your best friends, too.
Welcome home to Siena Farms, Rory."

## About Siena Farms

Farmer Chris Kurth, James Beard Award-winning Chef/Restaurant owner Ana Sortun and their daughter Siena live at Siena Farms in Sudbury, Massachusetts. Siena Farms is a family farm, growing over 100 varieties of vegetables for sale through Community Supported Agriculture (CSA) farm shares, area restaurants, and farm stores in Boston.Committed to sustainable agricultural practices; free of chemical herbicides, pesticides, and synthetic fertilizers, Siena Farms is a magical home to Siena and her best friends Rory, Agnes and Legacy. More information about Siena Farms can be found at SienaFarms.com

## About the Author

Author Lyndon Haviland is respected as a global leader, speaker and storyteller. She is a passionate advocate for human rights and is dedicated to bringing individuals and organizations together to achieve lasting social change. *A New Best Friend at Siena Farms* is a joyful outcome of her friendship with Chef Ana, Farmer Chris and their family. It is her second children's book. Learn more at LyndonHaviland.com

## About the Illustrator

Sarah Neff is an illustrator and artist with a long-standing love for characters and storytelling. She lives in Seattle. Learn more at Sarah-Neff.com

Printed in the USA
CPSIA information can be obtained
at www.ICGtesting.com
LVHW072139290923

759618LV00015B/206